MY SPIRITUAL JOURNEY

RODNEY HILLAIRE

Archway Publishing books may be ordered through booksellers or by contacting:

Archway Publishing
1663 Liberty Drive
Bloomington, IN 47403
www.archwaypublishing.com
844-669-3957

ISBN: 978-1-6657-1279-8 (sc)
ISBN: 978-1-6657-1278-1 (hc)
ISBN: 978-1-6657-1280-4 (e)

Print information available on the last page.

Archway Publishing rev. date: 11/24/2021

MY SPIRITUAL JOURNEY

Respect to all my sisters and brothers with peace, love to all and to Lummi
KEEP MY FIRES BURNING STRONG

My Totem Red Eagle Vision
Rodney Hillaire
May 6, 2013

BEAR

O Si'am e ne schal e che
ne-skli' kwenes sqwal e kw'kw'in-ol sqwal.
etie kyes Si'am e ne schal e che.
su'i't sen ohi'leq kwenes ena' tachel e'ti'e kyes
_____ (Tse) (Se) ne sna
ow'sen xe'chi't tsoux Xwlemi'chosen
i'u totestsen kwenes twn okwlth Si'am
tl'a'e'shen tsoux Xwlemi ena' tachel
tl'e Smi'lhe la'tse T'amxw'iq'sen.
hy'sh'qe Si'am e ne schal e che, Si'am
kwenes xwi'an, ne qwo qwel Si'am.

My dear friends and relatives.
I would like to say a few words, just a few words
today my friends and relatives.
It's true I'm happy to see you here today.
(name) male female my name
I don't understand the Lummi Language
But I'm trying to learn. My Friends.
I want to invite you here to Lummi
to a party there at Gooseberry Point.
Thank you my friends and relatives, my friends.
For listening to my words, my friends.

Month	Xwlemi'chosen	Picture	Qr code	English
August				Canoe words to learn
August	O Sii'am ne schaleche			Welcome canoe family Honorable friend
August				You are welcome to come ashore
August				Thank you my honorable friends
August				
August				We thank you for coming to our territory
August				Be careful in your journey with this sacred paddle
August	Hy'kwe'che e ne schaleche			Good bye my honorable friends
August	Ena'-lh etse Lhal tl'e tse en schtengexwen			We request to come ashore on your land
August	x'a-x'alh sqemel			We are continuing on our sacred paddle
August	Hy'kwe'che e ne schaleche			Good bye my friends and family
August	Kwai'kwi i' etoteng			We are hungry and tired
August	Ne stli ongest-t tse Stilem I'tse qweilsih			We want to share some songs and dances with you
	Ne stli ongest-t tse sxwiyam			We want to share stories with you
August	Qaqweng etse en schtengexwen			We want to rest on your land
August	'ey tsens 'ist			You're stroke is good

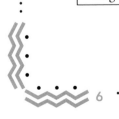

Month	Xwlemi'chosen	Picture	Qr code	English
August	cheqwost cen snexwlh			Bail out canoe
August	isteng			Pulling together
August	cho o'olh			Everyone in the canoe
August	tsi'qlho			Pacer in the front strokeman
August				Strong puller in the middle
August				skipper
August	Hy'sh'qe etse			Thank you for your hospitality
August	Hy'sh'qe etse s-lhen			Thank you for the meals
August				Paddles in
August				Paddles out
August	Kwel ilhen			Time to eat
August	cheli'qws			switch
August	yuan			forward
August	itl'a'-als i'qeqanelh			Backward and slow
August	ist lhexwsha tl'aqt			30 long pulls
August	c ist lhexwsha h'ch'eyetl			20 short pulls
August	ch'islan tse seli stilem			Hear the spirit sings
August	Che Xwlemi-lh_____tse ne sna			We are from___ My name is____
August	Ew't'ayeq t'iwilh ol etse kwaateng			Don't get mad just pray to the waters
August	Sat'se'sen tse sqemel			Raise paddles in the air

Keep My Fires Burning

Paddle Together Like the Wings of Eagles

Canoe Culture and Spiritual and by Ya Mentin

Rodney Hillaire

Lummi Culture Commission approved by book for Culture Awareness

Blessings of
Rodney Hillaire
By Rodney Hillaire

Lot of good canoe journeys
Lot of good visions, on ancient waters prayers on canoeing

Acknowledgement

I thank Rebecca, Justin and Julia, Systems of Care for helping make this possible. Spiritually, I thank my Mother.

Thanks for my Dad the Teaching Richard Jr Hillaire Canoe
Mommir's Mary M.
Fran N. Emit O. Edgre C. etc.
With Love and Respects of important Rojos who started canoe journeys.

Blessings of Rodney Hillaire

God loves us through our ancestors hope. Do something good for our people. As I realize when I feel bad and/or sad I pray for the one that cannot make the canoe journey, my racing buddies, elders, family, friends, Lummi, alcoholics, addicts and hope for the youth.

I think because they say if you're good on the journey you will receive a vision for your people; Because God loves us through our ancestors.

As I found a picture at the old tribal office from the late 1970's at the blue building. First thought was Sarah James, she used to drive a car all by herself. She was one of the elders there to support writing the Lummi Language alphabet and dictionary. After I got out of prison I had Rheumatoid Arthritis, and it gave me a bad leg. Elders and I used to race to the double doors, and the elders use to beat me; they used to say "your back" meaning back home.

So I thought about how God's will helped our people so I prayed to bless them as they blessed me. And I said "let it be God's will" so I looked up at the sun and it looked radiant like sparkles was around the sun light.

So I thought God heard me and I thought I'm going to change because of my bad leg. So I also prayed for a sign from heaven. Then I had thoughts put in my head "you will help your people and other peoples tribe" and I said again "let God's will be done, even good and bad." I cried after I thought about this prayer and Sarah James. She whispered, "Glad you remembered us!"

Elders the moon gave shape for a hand drum

Elder the flute came from the top of an old cedar tree with holes which made a good sound when the wind blew.

[Family History]

By Aunty Eve told me and my family about sacred waters north of San Juan Islands is ancient waters which has no name but give a walk of life. From Dad our ancestors paddled from Alaska to California, kidnapping females.

From Aunt Margret Hillarie had a war canoe party 300 years ago which annihilated the Sooke Tribe of Vancouver Island. Now our elders are asking peace.

From Dad Joseph Hillarie Grandpa carved totem poles all over the work and made a canoe sbi yo "sly fox" and long houses builder. Dad was undefeated war canoe racer because he invented the long stroke on the Red Wing canoe.

From Aunty Pauline and Margret Hay Tu Luk Frank Hillaire Great Grandfather save our culture I use to hear which Mayor and President came to town and they danced down the street and like it and started the parade. Dad was a carpenter and fisherman plus Kodiak and black bear hunter elk and deer hunter with rifle and archery. By Aunty Margret Lummi of Matt Paul had a whale canoe last killed a while 1877 by Samish and Anacortes area.

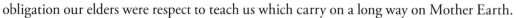

obligation our elders were respect to teach us which carry on a long way on Mother Earth.

God Bless through my spiritual journey all our Elders with all their wisdom and history by our ancestors. Keeping our schlangen for all of Lummi.

[Family Remedies]

Dad arthritis a rounded thick five inch grey furry leaf, skunk cabbage all wars dandelions white sap. Mothers birth 2-4 feet sticker bush plant by using this purpose top flower child birthing.

Uncle Gordon Wilson infection white birch tree by its bark inside put the inside bark in the sun 15 minutes or so then it turn white then use on wound. History use to be Indian ice cream with berries, been wiped out during settlers which was healthy.

Tribal arthritis – skunk cabbage

Grandmother and Aunty Margret use to make dip nets with nettle stems.

Dad leaned to make a deer call with two think sticks with grassy something thin in the middle which makes a high pitched whistle and low tone try to make love call.

Helen and Gordon water stick you'll find in a small water pond its good on a hot day.

At the age of 14 I moved from California to Lummi to live with Aunty Helen and Uncle Gordon Wilson. I used to walk to the Lummi Education Center. George Adams was the Teacher and Principal. George started the Lummi alphabet and dictionary. He taught with the Elders below the tribal offices at the Blue Building. In order to teach what the Lummi Language was like George would use birds or other animals.

I would eat my lunch with them by serving meals and drinks. They would have me say grace. I couldn't give some of the elders their drinks because their hands were shaky so they couldn't hold their drink. Those elders would get jealous because they would have to go to the dining room.

Then I went another way; fishing, racing canoe and attending the smokehouse.

I went fishing with Gabe Jefferson. He and I were herring fishing outside of Lummi Island. While pulling up to the fish buyer, I had not noticed him slip between the boats. He was wearing rain gear and wool. I noticed the boat rocking one way. I turned, jumped and grabbed him. He was a 340 pound man. Luckily I was strong enough to hold on to him. Someone saw us and yelled "man over board!" They helped get a hose line around him to use the boats wench to pull from the water to safety on the deck. Some days later I was praying for calm waters and plenty of seaweed fishing, because at that time there were 4 foot swells and white caps. I was deck hand and Gabe said "Rodney, look up!" As I did, the waters were calm and flat, it looked like glass.

First I canoed raced with my elders. They would show me how to canoe paddle, like my Dad did. I was taught by doing long pulls not to hit the paddle or the canoe because the cedar is alive, it's like hitting your own arm. They taught us how to canoe paddle quietly so they couldn't hear us coming. I would work out, speed punching the heavy bags, or kicking it. I would do this for two or three hours then I would run, in my boots, all the way to the Stommish Grounds and practice with four or five 12-man canoe clubs.

I believe I could have broken the World's Record time for fastest one minute mile, 3 minutes 27 seconds. Jimmie John Jr., (Lawrence) would time and watch his mileage on his Ford car as I ran.

First my song to start with three angels a appeared inside saying God going to sing a son after he sang I prayed please translate he said. I love my way, I love my way, God Cleanse me from all my sins. Ancient waters gave walk of life of our ancestors.

Plus I have our family history and Indian medicine handed down. And we should be faithfully praying and love one another and I heard it's like were in the state were facing the Ten Commandments of the Bible. Like I honored and respected a lot before their time going to Indian country heaven. First my Mom believed in me and my Dad gifted me canoeing. Dad was trying to make me an elder before I was an elder.

Therefore I still pray the spirit of Hay Tu Luk and the great white cloud Jesus Mary Mercy and redemption and consuming fire with pure thoughts and good words while Jesus at the right hand which starts to heal or gifted I pray for gifts through traditional arts and crafts family culture etc. which makes a better life and clean and sober through smokehouses not to heal them do it the right way for smokehouse. Peaceful Lummi life it goes a long way. I hope someone else becomes a prayer warrior.

By chance tradition would go hand and hand with our while culture with paddle shirt or dress, learning to walk in both worlds. Its our scared plastic. Also the news said drugs going down the facility drain causing harm to the fish and their eggs.

Keep My Fires Burning

Back to a vision I had of Hay Tu Luk doing hungry bear dance telling me he's hungry for fish and he's telling us we are hungry for the right of culture and traditions. Or I should say we're paddling together as we're hunger for the right of culture and tradition.

BEAR

A while ago Gini Cagey gave a picture of Great Grandpa in his paddle shirt which I learned again about paddle shirts. It started long time ago on the island only a few people could wear them and Hillarie's were one of them.

Also it would bring special memories for our elders; it reminds them of our history through their younger days.

I pray for our family elders and for Lummi to revive our culture to when Hay Tu Luk saved our culture, like the way it used to be. The Great Spirit.

I was told that I worked out more than a Marine. I enjoyed running long distances; I would run on the beach from the Fisherman's Cove to the Stommish Grounds to help with my canoe pulling training. My training began at the "old gym" (Lummi Neighborhood Facility) where I would work out then I would run to practices in the evenings at the Stommish Grounds.

Asides from fishing and canoe, I used to go the Smokehouse for two or three winters. I would split logs into four pieces, four foot logs and tend the fire. There were two big fires in the smoke house, I helped keep them burning. Keeping the house warm, it was good for the elders. I used to hear songs coming from the "big house" and would go down there, it would be pitch black out and there was no body down there.

Start Canoeing

I first was going to Tacoma Indian Center where I knew Connie McCloud, and talked to Phil Red Eagle at the center. I was told by the counselor from the center that Connie needed pullers for the Canoe Journey. During the Paddle to LaPush, 1997 I was photographed in the Seattle Times with our canoe family after having had paddled 50 miles to La Push because while leaving the Vancouver Island Strait we got caught in 9 foot swells, I remember the water being very cold and it was hard to see. One of our crew members Holly B., was scared to death and screaming. I was trying to help her make sure she was alright. Our tow support boat was going slow but the canoe carried us thought the rough sea. The Paddle to La Push was filled with my tests of strength, faith and courage. One time Connie and I were shopping and lightning struck no more than five feet away from us; it was very loud.

The Paddle to La Push gave many teaching to revitalize our cultural teachings. Leaders, Elders, skippers, community and children were sharing our ways. Phil Red Eagle got us carving tools for paddles and paddles for shirts, since Connie sewed my velvet burgundy shirt together. We had our ceremonial wool shirts for our canoe family, Thunder Spirit. This one time Connie was watching her grandson Manual and other children playing in a lake, sitting on a log and he was playing the skipper.

I vow to pray for our people, sx'wo'le and now for peace for our people. Like God would have someone be interpreted my talk about sx'wo'le reef net.

Days before Seattle news announced toxic waste was dumped in South Seattle for 14 years and was fined big time in south Salish Sea. One day we had a circle with Natural Resources Commission, Coash Salish Mini University; activists knew for a while there was bad fish so she tied herself to a Bellingham Oil Barge to stop an oil shipment. So I said God put us there for a purpose. There was a map I found earlier at Lummi that year I asked about it and sure enough it turned out to be theirs. I asked elders about plastic going down, later that year local news reported that fleece is getting in our water more than they thought from our laundry. They said Alaskan Chain of Aleutian Islands found didn't know Lummi Language word "sx'wo'le." What he said to me, commit me. And I did tell Uncle I could hear sx'wo'le in the wind and hear people arguing that's years after I say Hay Tu Luk in the hungry bear dance and it was also years before the ancestors community burning.

We're asking the Creator for our reef netting in a peaceful way in the right passage. When I pulled canoe I praying to the water for our people, my ancestors and Hay Tu Luk and Jesus. And earned respect from my Mom and Dad with canoeing, paddle shirts and spiritual God song.

Remember telling Troy and Shirley Hay Tu Luk is before our time. Ain't we like family, Coast Salish. We the people will recognize his dream and vision.

As the other children were paddling. I witnessed our teachings being handed down to our younger generations who were watching and learning from our journey together.

Connie McCloud assisted me, in canoe coordinating. To share the teachings, I said "Leave the bad thoughts and bad ways on shore. We pray, pray to the water. We laugh, joke and sing together on the canoe." I reminded that we need a good pacer in the front, the power house in the middle of the canoe and a good responsible skipper. Also, that we must always pull straight with the canoe and not bang or hit the paddle on the canoe because the cedar is alive and when we sing our paddle songs to make sure the water and canoe hear us sing.

Puyallup is like my second family. Jeff Smith skippered at times. We used to paddle 30-60 miles a day. We would get up two hours before sun rise and leave early to get to our destination by sunset. It was peaceful. We would joke, laugh, pray and sing. We use to hear spirits sing out in the water, like they were happy to see us.

We used to practice at Tacoma Harbor. Then finally it was time for Paddle to Puyallup. I remember passing Lummi, and I was singing my "God Song" out loud, and Albert Combs heard me singing and said that it was the paddle song. Connie use to say "If you're doing it for your people it will be a peaceful journey."

Once while preparing for tribal journey, we was asked by the Tulalip and Port Gamble S'kallum Tribes to teach their youth about canoeing. It was a hay day. We easily had about 160 tribal youth during that evening, before the Paddle to Tulalip.

I also learned about sacredness and beliefs while on canoe journeys. For example, Makah Elder Mary taught that holding hands wasn't permitted unless married. Otherwise, the male and female would hold on to the opposite ends of a cedar stick instead. Also I heard the teaching that if you are injured or very tired or sore that you are not to help carry or pack the canoe because the canoe wants only the strong people to help.

Plus I like the beauty of song and dance of their nature, of their country where they come from or sometimes they use smoke house and some mask dance and song. No cameras.

I used to be a extra puller for Squamish and the would honor me for being a strong and respectful. So they would let me sing with them during protocols.

Hay Tu Luk said "Go home," so I packed up and went home. I did a Spiritual Journey and Canoe Journey story about how to change for the better. Go to school and working after institutionalization. Spirits are real, think and do well, pray. You will be an Elder one day and may have a vision from the ancestors that you have to interpret in your own way.

A Narcotics Anonymous presentation was provided to the San Juan sx'wo'le. What was said and prayed for were prayer songs for our youth, sx'wo'le, Troy Olsen and Shirley Williams' safe passage. I felt the spirits were present and they were glad. As if the spirits were saying with us "we are here at this present place."

Also I asked them to pray for all they're doings, teachings and what they are trying to do. While I blessed them with my song, "I love my way, I love my way! God cleanse me from all my sins!" I explained to them that it's the Creator's song to share. I prayed for powerful people.

I did remember an Elder say to me that if I ever see Hay Tu Luk that I am to interpret it in my own way.

I talked to Smitty about prophesying sx'wo'le. He said one could not do it on their own years ago, and that you had to be an Elder. Elders were typically the ones that had visions. Plus I were being set up to God, Hay Tu Luk and Sx'wo'le.

I wrote a letter; in my letter were my prayers for culture, tradition and fish. I also reflected to when I met Hay Tu Luk. It was a few years before a community burning. Elders were praying and having ceremony for the return of sx'wo'le. During this ceremony I could hear voices arguing. I felt left out, but I remember my Dad and Elden saying that I could not do it on my own, so I kept praying on it for the ancestors to provide me with wisdom.

The next year, I made my first wool blanket, and then I prayed towards the San Juan Islands, offering blessings for Shirley Williams, the sx'wo'le and Hay Tu Luk. I heard from Hay Tu Luk, that Shirley would be calling, and she did. I didn't have my phone on but the next morning at 5:30 I received a message from Shirley Williams.

I had a vision of a hill, and later it came true while skippering to Cowichan in Duncan, British Columbia. I was recognized by my Mom, Dad, Grandmother and Hay Tu Luk the first day at San Juan Island. I also prayed to Hay Tu Luk a few other times, he replied, like would call their be meetings couple times at San Juan Islands and one time Great Great Grandfather would reply, she would call and said go home.

Paddle to Lummi 2007

I helped with transportation between the Stommish Grounds, Wex'liem Community Building and camps. I made sure guest had cold drinks, and would teach our tribal youth to make sure the elders sitting in the protocol tent had cold drinks. I helped look out for any first aid matters that needed attention, i.e., I helped a women who had swollen feet get first aid treatment. During protocol I stood and danced with my Hillarie family, even though I had been up really early and working really late, helping with Paddle to Lummi.

Lummi Protocol – Hillaire Family

Paddle to Quinault (Taholah, WA) 2002

When we left Makah, and on the Hoh River, I thought we were 1 mile or so, just before Quinault we were late and it was getting foggy, within a mile from shore and then we could hear the wave's, so we decided to go towards the waves and cliffs, our canoe swamped from the waves. Lucky we were wearing life vests and holding onto the canoe and we were in the water for 20 to 30 minutes. Connie McCloud was holding on to me and I was trying to stay above water. We all ended getting hypothermia. My brother saw us in the news. Said it was reported that we were missing by the Coast Guards and getting late and foggy and that we were seen by support crews. They had included a picture of our canoe family on the news report.

When we finally made it to shore, they had open cabins prepared for us, that were heated, showers and blankets ready. The team of Emergency Responders, CPN's and RN's were nearby and came to help us. After we all were safe and rested, we had to do healing work for our canoe family. Shaker Church members from Queets came to offer their work, songs and prayers for us. Some of our canoe family didn't return to the canoe for the rest of the journey, some of us just went with ground transportation to Taholah.

The Muckleshoot Healing Journey was hard for many of the youth at times, having to pull 20 to 30 mile distances. During this particular journey I experienced a miracle. I called Shirley Williams twice and there was a meeting through the next two days. I prayed for peace and safety for the canoe journey, after trying to publish my spiritual book for the youth about cultural awareness and teachings. It was blowing and raining, and I could hear screaming and crying. I opened my door to go outside and my instincts were telling me something was wrong and later that day the news reported that Paris was attacked. A little while after a loud voice said to me in my living room of my apartment, "Your book will make peace for our people." The loud voice I heard was a young upstanding good man. At first I felt fear, but I knew it was meant for good, good prayers and good heart; that my prayers

To Whom It May Concern:

I am writing to you to ask your permission to request a cedar log, this log will be carved into a traveling canoe. I will be carving this cedar log with other people from the community. We have a few canoes at Lummi that will be used a model for this project. I have talked to a people from the community and the suggested that I turn to you for guidance. I understand that the tribe has some cedar logs that may work for this project. If not I can use a tree that may have fell itself in the woods.

This canoe will be carefully monitored while in construction and will be ready for the 2018 canoe journey to Puyallup. This has been one of my passions for many years; I have been involved in the canoe journey since the early stages.

I believe that the cedar canoe made from one log is much more traditional that the strip canoes that are being made today as well as the fiber glass ones, I feel this project will help build a unity in our canoe families and will be one that can build a lifelong learning experience.

Pleases contact me as to when this be discussed at the cultural committee meeting, I know there will be lots of planning to make this a reality. Together we can make it happen.

Hy'sh'qe
Yamentin
Rodney Hillaire

I was driving...no, he was driving; I was riding with him, down Chief Ironwood towards the hill, up Scott Road. I said, "Dad, I have a vision. I see three angels. They say God's going to sing a song to me. (*Singing, "Hello h'huh huh uhhuhuh/Hello, h'huh, uh huhuhuh/Oheyahey Yaheyahey, Aheyahey"*) He goes "Sing it! Sing it! Sing it! Sing it!" over and over and over and over.

And I prayed that he would translate it. I told my Dad. He says "It means, translated, 'Lummi way, Lummi way, God take me from all my sins." He kept saying, "Remember that song–sing it, sing it, sing it, sing it!"

Then I had a vision of Jesus in a sweat lodge. I was with a counselor and a young medicine man. She lived up near Crab Bay–the mouth of the Nooksack River. She had a sweat lodge, and was dating a native medicine man from Canada.

Anyway, we were back in his flat after a couple rounds, and he said "Your eyes are closed?"

And we both said "Yeah," me and my counselor.

"Open them." And Jesus was sitting in there. He had his white cloak, and white spirit. He had his crown of thorns. He had love in his eyes. It was...there was just that peace, that gaaaaa, you know, wow!

But before that I used to pray with turmoil. I was bothered with a called Djidjis–Death. That was why I was with the counselor. I asked for a sign–and that was my sign! That was really healing, so I went to an institution, traveled, with money. And that's when I read my story of my judgment–monitor, my preacher called it "Monitor". I called it "Book of Life" or monitoring my thoughts and memories. Like an angel was telling me parts of my life, and I was writing it down. Every time I quit I stepped right back up where I left off. Yes!

I wrote some visions...I don't remember that.

One time I had a vision at my Dad's house, too. This white cloud appeared. I woke up and the whole room was all lit like a cloud, glowing in the whole room. There was a spirit came out. I didn't recognize him, but like he was a little totem, but he was walking. And kind of some other visions.

I used to go to Church with my Mom. I used to talk to her. She was telling me to pray for my bad feelings. We talked about the Bible a little bit. She thought I had my visions coming in, and I did. I tried to learn about the [name] fire, as it appeared, like something was going to happen.

I lost my two brothers to Shannon and Marietta–I lost Matthew and Albert, and I lost Kelly and that whole house. I lost my brother Albert. My Mom and Dad.

When we came down we'd have a lot of canoe journeys. I used to pray to Jesus on canoe journeys because I remember a lot of my history, how my ancestors started out, my Dad used to tell me. My ancestors used to travel from Mid-Alaska to California kidnapping females. They used to go like a hundred miles at a time. No seats–they were on their knees and paddling.

I taught the Puyallup how to canoe. I taught canoe for about almost eight or nine years, then I moved back to Lummi. Puyallup had the culture and the language again. I taught them how to pace, how to power up, pull. The skipper's got to be positive, make sure everybody leaves the bad stuff on shore, for when hearts are all together, good things happen.

There was a lady, too, Mary McClellan. She was Makah. She was a cultural canoe specialist, an elder there who knew a lot about all the canoe territories.

Visions. I had a vision of my Red Eagle (*Holds up a black pen sketch on white paper, of a bald eagle, face forward, view from underneath, semi-rectangular wings with a slight U-curve typical of eagles and widening at the tips, each wing subdivided into three rectangles, the head/body/tail forming a rounded, upward-pointing triangle.*) Uncle Gary Heytulik had an eagle, Mary L. Cagey–Lummi Eagle. Some tribes have eagles. Some tribes have an eagle *and* a whale. I had those ones, but the Eagle has been at my side. I recognize that there's power behind it, I guess.

And before Uncle Penny passed away, we used to be out at a lot of burnings up there. You had to be there *early* in the morning; I think it was like six o'clock, five o'clock? Driving down the road up Rodney's Story.

I'm going to do my story. I've been very stubborn *[laughter]* from when I was young. Do that now or later?

"It's up to you. We have time for it. We can do it now or we can do it later."

Do some of it? Okay.

To begin my story, my first memory was Marietta. I was just a kid. I left there when I was six years old.

I moved to California. I went to Banning, along the Sierras north of Palm Springs. Then we moved to Palm Springs.

Just before I was seven I'd seen a boy's club camp. Boy's club–what they call the core boys and girls level. I wanted to be in there, and I got to be there when I turned seven *[laugh]*. We used to go camping in the mountains, ten mile hike, horse riding, We even had shooting twenty-two rifles, whatever. Field games, swimming, sailing.

I had some cousins that lived there, too, most of their lives, while we were there: Auntie Tours, Tony and Randy, I remember. They were my cousins; they were my mother's family, with us. They were Viet Nam veterans, Tony and Randy. They were big guys, scary guys you don't want to know, heh heh. They were in tank in Viet Nam, running over mine fields. We used to go camping out in the desert, watching them practice blowing up jeeps and tanks [laughs].

I met some famous people there. My brothers and sisters knew them more because they were about their age. The guy who invented a rifle, a thirty-foot rifle with a ten foot scope, that could shoot something two miles away, see like a can and take a shoot, and it takes about a minute or so, and then it disappears. *[laugh]_* There was a bus driver and air-brakes inventor. There were mostly millionaires in Palm Springs, movie stars like Jerry Lewis, [*Rock Holme?*], Chuck Connors, I've seen him, Liberace, heh, six-million dollar man–Lee Majors. Howard Hughes was the millionaire; you could recognize him because he would always wear suit and ties, heh heh.

We used to go to this...I used to climb this mountain a couple times, when I was a kid, They have Arrow Tramway cable-cars, three inches thick, four hundred feet long, something like that, three hundred foot cliff. Cable car. We'd go out there and have lunch, play in the snow. It was a luxury–we had swimming pools, slushes *[laugh]*. And really, after that, because of my sister's brother-in-law, Ricky, we used to go swimming all day long, or we'd bicycle all day long, cross-town. *[laugh]* We used to make choppers out of them.

And then my Mom divorced–my Mom and Dad, and I kind of lived in Palm Springs and up here in Whatcom County, back and forth, flying since I was eight years old, so a couple years, a couple times. I lived with my Dad up here. He had horses. And then I moved back to California.

Then I moved back home when I was fourteen. I lived with my Auntie Helen. I learned about herbs and plants, then. Uncle Gordon knew a lot. I forgot some of what he said.

We used to walk to school for five miles. The Lummi Education Center, we used to call it. There was this plant. We used to walk down on hot summer days and peel the bark off. It grows in water–water you can't drink. It's like a celery, with a water component. You just peel the bark off and eat it when you're thirsty. It's good for you on a long walk.

At the Lummi Ed Center George Adams was the principal and teacher, and there were some elders. Below the school, in the blue building, we used to have an adult/child block, which was an old naval base. We had Joe Hillaire–Joseph Hillaire's theory of Lummi language. His theory went with him in the grave. His writings, his dictionary. We learned that, for the French language, like "X" goes "hwoo" in French; in Lummi it's chhhkh. Really changed the concept. We started learning alphabets, inventing them. He used me as a guinea-pig to teach more students, trying to sound them out alphabetically. There'd be like twenty-four alphabets, vowels. We studied them in birds and animals, speech. *[At 0:09:44 Rodney speaks in the Lummi language, which I don't know how to spell.]* That's another way of saying, "I am here. I am Lummi. I am here to say a few good words, make other friends and others."

Then I went fishing. I went, I tried to go to school in Bellingham. When I moved from California I was, like, two years ahead of everybody, from the rich people's school, coming back to Lummi and Bellingham. My mother put me in a grade below kids my age, instead of kids that were older. I got really disappointed–heartbroken. I didn't want to do it over again. So life was hard, because my Mom and Dad were not too traditional, because they went to Chumallah Indian Boarding School. But they could learn a lot of good things. They'd try and inspire me.

I went to institutions–jail. By that time I was praying for a good life. I had this girlfriend; her name was Toodlelee Solomon. Her nickname was Toodlelee. She was going to have my kid, and she died. That turned my life all the way around again. It went sour–turmoil.

But when I went to jail, it was like God told me I was going to go there. I remembered places I've seen in the jail. I'd had a vision; it was one of the first visions to happen. It had a red eagle first. I had a vision of six sacred colors. Blue leader, red power, yellow dignity, orange juice, green wisdom, purple spirit.

I always thought God was watching me. He judged me, told me of my life. I read in a book, too, experiences when they passed away, he recorded a light, just like a recording monitor: thoughts and memories, like imaginary things you think when you're a kid, things you did in life. He was watching me all the time, ever since I was a kid. I'm going to share that in my story.

And then I saw, the time I was with my Dad, I know I should say prayers for him. I went to Montana. I went to Job Corps. I couldn't complete it because of alcohol. But I was involved with forest firefighting school training–school testing, mainly, because we started: we were the first students of the forest firefighting Montana run and fire department. They were choosing me as a lead person, how to control the fire and have several places, to recognize good places for paratroopers and firefighters to be. Cowlitz Fire was one of the things I did.

But I had a brother, Kelly, who was a forest firefighter; he was really a good boy. He had masonry experience, and was a carpenter and fisherman. My brother, Albert, he graduated and went into the military. They were both football players, semi-pro. Me, I played football in junior high. When I came to Lummi I started canoe-racing for about almost four years.

And we lived in Seattle for a couple years, with Uncle Penny and Val Layette. I think Uncle Gordon would soon be there, and Helen. I was just a kid then, a couple years there. We went to visit the Space Needle. *(laugh)* It used to be cheap in those days. *(laugh)*

I started fishing. My first time fishing was a hairy experience. Gabe Jefferson–I went fishing for him. It'd be like three or four o'clock in the morning. My first job–fishing job. I gave him breakfast before we'd go out. I saved his life.

We were at a fish-buyer. We were next to him, and I was cleaning the deck when the boat jerked. He called my name. I turned around and I grabbed him by the armpits, because he was sinking down. He was like two hundred pounds, but he had his wetsuit and wool, so he was like three hundred pounds. The boat was like that *(gestures, showing a downward angle)* halfway angled. I tried to haul him up. I yelled "Man overboard!" and they finally got a hoist–the fish-buying boat–and put it around his arms and winched him up. That was scary for my first years! *(laughs.)* I was young.

I used to fish, two couple weeks straight. I'd sleep an hour a night, come in maybe for food and fuel. I'd kind of doze night and day, from Francis's Bellingham site.

After my Auntie showed me to bathe in the water, my Dad used to take me to smokehouses on Crab Day. Sam Cagey would hold them, so they could all call. I would receive a song, and my Dad would make ties for each of our relationships; they were forgiving things we all did.

Past Little Bear, going by the Stommish Grounds, you could see spirit like dark clouds walking up towards the fire, *[laugh]* up the hill, coming from the Stommish Grounds when I was driving. I'd think, "Oh no, those are spirits! They got to me! I have to go out and where I'm going later I had a vision of hay tu luk I was walking in front of aunty Helens house then I heard my name called Rodney then I looked to my right I saw Frank Hillaire do the hungry bear dance then I look around saw fishing nets I thought fish then I heard uncle not my fish it was to pray for our fish not to go bad like I pray for culture tradition and our fish months later I came back I thought reef net and people arguing like vow silence in prayer he also in paddle shirt then I heard Dana Wilson name so paddle to Puyallup 1999 then I had a vision of a hill I look for it for years then I skippered to Cowichen and stop at Shaw island then left the next day there's my vision it was Orcas Island I screamed and yawed this was my vision truely.

Rodney's Story.

I'm going to do my story. I've been very stubborn *[laughter]* from when I was young. Do that now or later?
"It's up to you. We have time for it. We can do it now or we can do it later."
Do some of it? Okay.
To begin my story, my first memory was Marietta. I was just a kid. I left there when I was six years old.
I moved to California. I went to Banning, along the Sierras north of Palm Springs. Then we moved to Palm Springs.

Just before I was seven I'd seen a boy's club camp. Boy's club–what they call the core boys and girls level. I wanted to be in there, and I got to be there when I turned seven *[laugh]*. We used to go camping in the mountains, ten-mile hike, horse riding, we even had shooting twenty-two rifles, whatever. Field games, swimming, sailing.

I had some cousins that lived there, too, most of their lives, while we were there: Auntie Joice Tours, Tony and Randy, I remember. They were my cousins; they were my mother's family, with us. They were Viet Nam veterans, Tony and Randy. They were big guys, scary guys you don't want to know, heh heh. They were in tank in Viet Nam, running over mine fields. We used to go camping out in the desert, watching them practice blowing up jeeps and tanks [laughs].

I met some famous people there. My brothers and sisters knew them more because they were about their age. The guy who invented a rifle, a thirty-foot rifle with a ten foot scope, that could shoot something two miles away, see like a can and take a shoot, and it takes about a minute or so, and then it disappears. *[laugh]_* There was a bus driver and air-brakes inventor. There were mostly millionaires in Palm Springs, movie stars like Jerry Lewis, *[Rock Holme?]*, Chuck Connors, I've seen him, Liberace, heh, six-million dollar man–Lee Majors. Howard Hughes was the millionaire; you could recognize him because he would always wear suit and ties, heh heh.

We used to go to this...I used to climb this mountain a couple times, when I was a kid, They have Arial??? Arrow Tramway cable-cars, three inches thick, four hundred feet long, something like that, three hundred foot cliff. Cable car. We'd go out there and have lunch, play in the snow. It was a luxury–we had swimming pools, slushes *[laugh]*. And really, after that, because of my sister's brother-in-law, Ricky, we used to go swimming all day long, or we'd bicycle all day long, cross-town. *[laugh]* We used to make choppers out of them.

And then my Mom divorced–my Mom and Dad, and I kind of lived in Palm Springs and up here in Whatcom County, back and forth, flying since I was eight years old, so a couple years, a couple times. I lived with my Dad up here. He had horses. And then I moved back to California.

Then I moved back home when I was fourteen. I lived with my Auntie Helen. I learned about herbs and plants, then. Uncle Gordon knew a lot. I forgot some of what he said.

We used to walk to school for five miles. The Lummi Education Center, we used to call it. There was this plant. We used to walk down on hot summer days and peel the bark off. It grows in water–water you can't drink. It's like a celery, with a water component. You just peel the bark off and eat it when you're thirsty. It's good for you on a long walk.

At the Lummi Ed Center George Adams was the principal and teacher, and there were some elders. Below the school, in the blue building, we used to have an adult/child block, which was an old naval base. We had Joe Hillaire–Joseph Hillaire's theory of Lummi language. His theory went with him in the grave. His writings, his dictionary. We learned that, for the French language, like "X" goes "hwoo" in French; in Lummi it's chhhkh. Really changed the concept. We started learning alphabets, inventing them. He used me as a guinea-pig to teach more students, trying to sound them out alphabetically. There'd be like twenty-four alphabets, vowels. We studied them in birds and animals, speech. *[At 0:09:44 Rodney speaks in the Lummi language, which I don't know how to spell.]* I know how to spell by heart once after, Smiths Chief and Luttie saw me write the speech. She said your not an Elder it broke my heart so I went a bad way. That's another way of saying, "I am here. I am Lummi. I am here to say a few good words, make other friends and others."

Then I went fishing. I went, I tried to go to school in Bellingham. When I moved from California I was, like, two years ahead of everybody, from the rich people's school, coming back to Lummi and Bellingham. My mother put me in a grade below kids my age, instead of kids that were older. I got really disappointed–heartbroken. I didn't want to do it over again. So life was hard, because my Mom and Dad were not too traditional, because they went to Chumallah Indian Boarding School. But they could learn a lot of good things. They'd try and inspire me.

I went to institutions–jail. By that time I was praying for a good life. I had this girlfriend; her name was Toodlelee Solomon. Her nickname was Toodlelee. She was going to have my kid, and she died. That turned my life all the way around again. It went sour–turmoil.

But when I went to jail, it was like God told me I was going to go there. I remembered places I've seen in the jail. I'd had a vision; it was one of the first visions to happen. It had a red eagle first. I had a vision of six sacred colors. Blue leader, red power, yellow dignity, orange juice, green wisdom, purple spirit.

I always thought God was watching me. He judged me, told me of my life. I read in a book, too, experiences when they passed away, he recorded a light, just like a recording monitor: thoughts and memories, like imaginary things you think when you're a kid, things you did in life. He was watching me all the time, ever since I was a kid. I'm going to share that in my story.

And then I saw, the time I was with my Dad, I know I should say prayers for him. I went to Montana. I went to Job Corps. I couldn't complete it because of alcohol. But I was involved with forest firefighting school training–school testing, mainly, because we started: we were the first students of the forest firefighting Montana run and fire department. They were choosing me as a lead person, how to control the fire and have several places, to recognize good places for paratroopers and firefighters to be. Cowlitz Fire was one of the things I did.

But I had a brother, Kelly, who was a forest firefighter; he was really a good boy. He had masonry experience, and was a carpenter and fisherman. My brother, Albert, he graduated and went into the military. They were both football players, semi-pro. Me, I played football in junior high. When I came to Lummi I started canoe-racing for about almost four years.

And we lived in Seattle for a couple years, with Uncle Penny and Valet Layette. I think Uncle Gordon would soon be there, and Helen. I was just a kid then, a couple years there. We went to visit the Space Needle. *(laugh)* It used to be cheap in those days. *(laugh)*

I started fishing. My first time fishing was a hairy experience. Gabe Jefferson—I went fishing for him. It'd be like three or four o'clock in the morning. My first job—fishing job. I gave him breakfast before we'd go out. I saved his life.

We were at a fish-buyer. We were next to him, and I was cleaning the deck when the boat jerked. He called my name. I turned around and I grabbed him by the armpits, because he was sinking down. He was like two hundred pounds, but he had his wetsuit and wool, so he was like three hundred pounds. The boat was like that *(gestures, showing a downward angle)* halfway angled. I tried to haul him up. I yelled "Man overboard!" and they finally got a hoist—the fish-buying boat—and put it around his arms and winched him up. That was scary for my first years! *(laughs.)* I was young.

I used to fish, two couple weeks straight. I'd sleep an hour a night, come in maybe for food and fuel. I'd kind of doze night and day, from Francis's Bellingham site.

After my Auntie showed me to bathe in the water, my Dad used to take me to smokehouses on Crab Bay. Sam Cagey would hold them, so they could all call. I would receive a song, and my Dad would make ties for each of our relationships; they were forgiving things we all did.

I was driving...no, he was driving; I was riding with him, down Chief Ironwood towards the hill, up Scott Road. I said, "Dad, I have a vision. I see three angels. They say God's going to sing a song to me. *(Singing, "Hello h'huh huh uhhuhuh/Hello, h'huh, uh huhuhuh/Oheyahey Yaheyahey, Aheyahey")* He goes "Sing it! Sing it! Sing it! Sing it!" over and over and over and over.

And I prayed that he would translate it. I told my Dad. He says "It means, translated, I Love My I Love My cleanse 'Lummi way, Lummi way, God take me from all my sins." He kept saying, "Remember that song—sing it, sing it, sing it, sing it!"

Then I had a vision of Jesus in a sweat lodge. I was with a counselor and a young medicine man. She lived up near Crab Bay—the mouth of the Nooksack River. She had a sweat lodge, and was dating a native medicine man from Canada.

Anyway, we were back in his flat after a couple rounds, and he said "Your eyes are closed?"
And we both said "Yeah," me and my counselor.
"Open them." And Jesus was sitting in there. He had his white cloak, and white spirit. He had his crown of thorns. He had love in his eyes. It was...there was just that peace, that gaaaaa, you know, wow!

But before that I used to pray with turmoil. I was bothered with a called Djidjis–Death. That was why I was with the counselor. I asked for a sign–and that was my sign! That was really healing, so I went to an institution, traveled, with money. And that's when I read my story of my judgment–monitor, my preacher called it "Monitor". I called it "Book of Life" or monitoring my thoughts and memories. Like an angel was telling me parts of my life, and I was writing it down. Every time I quit I stepped right back up where I left off. Yes!

I wrote some visions...I don't remember that.

One time I had a vision at my Dad's house, too. This white cloud appeared. I woke up and the whole room was all lit like a cloud, glowing in the whole room. There was a spirit came out. I didn't recognize him, but like he was a little totem, but he was walking. And kind of some other visions.

I used to go to Church with my Mom. I used to talk to her. She was telling me to pray for my bad feelings. We talked about the Bible a little bit. She thought I had my visions coming in, and I did. I tried to learn about the [name] fire, as it appeared, like something was going to happen.

I lost my two brothers to Shannon and Marietta–I lost Matthew and Albert, and I lost Kelly and that whole house. I lost my brother Albert. My Mom and Dad.

When we came down we'd have a lot of canoe journeys. I used to pray to Jesus on canoe journeys because I remember a lot of my history, how my ancestors started out, my Dad used to tell me. My ancestors used to travel from Mid-Alaska to California kidnapping females. They used to go like a hundred miles at a time. No seats–they were on their knees and paddling.

I taught the Puyallup how to canoe. I taught canoe for about almost eight or nine years, then I moved back to Lummi. Puyallup had the culture and the language again. I taught them how to pace, how to power up, pull. The skipper's got to be positive, make sure everybody leaves the bad stuff on shore, for when hearts are all together, good things happen.

There was a lady, too, Mary McClellan. She was Makah. She was a cultural canoe specialist, an elder there who knew a lot about all the canoe territories.

Visions. I had a vision of my Red Eagle *(Holds up a black pen sketch on white paper, of a bald eagle, face forward, view from underneath, semi-rectangular wings with a slight U-curve typical of eagles and widening at the tips, each wing subdivided into three rectangles, the head/body/tail forming a rounded, upward-pointing triangle.)* Uncle Gary Hillarie had an eagle, Mary L. Cagey–Lummi Eagle. Some tribes have eagles. Some tribes have an eagle *and* a whale. I had those ones, but the Eagle has been at my side. I recognize that there's power behind it, I guess.

And before Uncle Penny passed away, we used to be out at a lot of burnings up there. You had to be there *early* in the morning; I think it was like six o'clock, five o'clock? Driving down the road up past Little Bear, going by the Stommish Grounds, you could see spirit like dark clouds walking up towards the fire, *[laugh]* up the hill, coming from the Stommish Grounds when I was driving. I'd think, "Oh no, those are spirits! They got to me! I have to go out and where I'm going later (33:00)

I had a vision of hay tu luk I was walking in front of aunty Helens house then I heard my name called Rodney.

Then I looked to my right I saw Frank Hillaire full regalia like the pictures you see do the hungry bear dance then I look around.

Saw fishing nets I thought fish then I heard uncle not my fish it was to pray for our fish not to go bad like I pray for culture tradition and our fish months later I came back I thought reef net and people arguing like vow silence in prayer he also in paddle shirt then 34:18 then I heard Dana Wilson name called, Tory I don't know if he was reef netter. I went to school with him in Bellingham.

Dana as a good guy he helped a lot, he helped himself so he could help others, clean, sober fisherman.

During my canoe journeys, I had a vision looked and looked 97 to 2008

Skippered 2007 which was the paddle to Lummi.

2008 was Cowichen, paddled across the San Juan Islands

Shaw Island then to Cowichen

Shaw island to Orcas

So really happy yelling, that was our ancestral lands

I had a vision to about something good, good bad

Pray for the east

I always like working with the youth after that

37:07 Katerie Indian saint became a saint in 2012 I think, Katerie Mohawk of Albequre, New York

At the graves, it said she was a Indian saint

My mom had good words about her

My mom was great but she was not recognized, she had powers

Like I said she recognized that person

She was always right

She said she would say??? pray and tell them to do something about it

38:19

My dad was a purse seiner

Deer hunter, riffle archery

So paddle to Puyallup 1999 then I had a vision of a hill I look for it for years then

Shaw Island then left the next day there's my vision

It was Orcas Island I screamed and yawed this was my vision truely

My story my name Ya Mentin is my dad was always saying our ansectors has traveled Alaska and to Califorina kidnapping females and always war partys and I learned history the hard way while back at Lummi stommish days Aunty Margret Greene and I said I was a with the Puyullup tribe with the canoe they got from the Sooke tribe Canada and it was morning after breakfast too reconize I am from Lummi tribe and my name is Rodney Hillaire then a man from Sooke said we like to kill the Hillaires and after I told aunty she said yeah we our ansectors annihilated then 300 hundred years ago any ways along time ago their was only a few men that could wear paddle shirts and Hillaires was one of them and before the paddles were on leather with the tribes had lots of different shapes and they represent their war clubs and Hillaires wear large paddles on their shirts plus the follow years people liked them and it beautiful plus some used the valvet from the French and Hillaires had more and many war clubs or the most paddles it shows our greatness and my great grandpa Frank Hillaire Hay tu lak which means He Bear we bear clan use to hide out at Makal tribe and keep our sacred ways a live and my dad was the greats canoe racer and were brabbing who was the greatest canoe puller and grand uncle Joseph Hillaire made a one racing canoe its name sly fox he also said it a moled model for the red wing and lone wolf and we use to take care of it for years when we were young he fix it up and let us kids take it out in the water plus it a model for a traveling canoe which I'm going to make and I got all the tools and my dad was the last traditional meat gather Elk DX Deer and Bear meat always in the freezer also was a carpenter and part time fishermen

Remembering my vision of Frank Hillaire Hay tru lay Hay tu lak he always recognize me before I go out our ancestors territory and he just sat 'go home' and my mom Dad and grandma also then I would say thank you four times and an inviy from Shirley and Troy we had a talken circle I was saying I found this salish sea map about preserving fish and plants and activists where their and iryed trying to say God put use theyre fe before going there on the news a Seattle man was find for fourteen years $1000.00s of dollars every years and out in the islands coastal salish on english camp an lime bay they had the 6 hundred foot long houses history and they showed us pictures that they took our Reef netersway of life also my spiritual growth I asked the kids to pray for the loved ones and some of them to pray for family and ansectors because of broke broken home sat sometimes the kids learn about marine life and before we took a mile walk in the woods I sang my God song I love my I love my way I love my way God cleans me from all my sins after I sang my vision mean and hungry which I translate hungry for culture.

This came from great grandpa vision waking up form end of winter mean and hungry

That was 2015 year and on our way to mucklesoot that year there was a healing journey at there at protocal I mc to the crowd we come here for a purpose I told the people our Lummi kid kidsa they learned about marine life and medicine plus food to preserve plus I told them I helped Westhire the other canoe journey and if a youth got mad I would sat go pray to the water and another journey I prayed to uncles for family bear mask and made me lonely because they too pee passed away and I couldn't go to Lummi protocol plus I was hungry we didn't have lunch and I was tired so I stayed home and a journey meeting Mary McQuillom had question of the coast salish eagle vision and aunty said they are all black face

Memories of passing elders Mart McQuilolim from Makah she tried to make me marry couple of her grand dearterts and all the elders were calling her master canoe spicelist because she knew the shape and what territory it came from also one canoe you can not carry if your tiereds or hurt arm and lag and other if your your not married the young couple can not hold hands our Lummi canoe good thoughts and good words but later Mery step down she tried to marry me one of her three grand dealters

Spicelty we were walking together with Frank Nalson Edger Charles RIP you would recognize the elders in Canada James Hoobucket Emit Oliver and the chief and all elders canoe carvers from all over coastal salish

All the elderer always in peace and confintend and ready the purpose to talk our wisdom to who needs and I most the only Lummi whom have all respect for all the tribes because my dad said do not have respect for the other tribes and and Candice told the youth Becky told me

Printed in the United States
by Baker & Taylor Publisher Services